Make Your Day

Five Things Successful People Do Before 8 a.m.

Michelle L Brown

ISBN-10: 154498605X
ISBN-13: 978-1544986050

DEDICATION

I would like to dedicate this book to Terri Savelle Foy, my coach, my mentor, my cheerleader. You taught me how to become more so I could be, do and have more, and for that I'm forever grateful to you!

CONTENTS

INTRODUCTION

So, you'd like to be successful. Maybe even *long to* be successful. But how do you get there? If the successes of people like Bill Gates leaves you in awe and maybe thinking, "I could never do that," think again. What is the only difference between the success-oriented crowd and those who are... not so much? It's so simple you might miss it if you're not paying attention. In fact, that's the problem. For most people who desire to make positive changes in their lives, it's not a mind-boggling IQ or genius powers that make the difference.

What the successful know that the average don't is *the power of habits*. Yep, that's it. Sorry to disappoint you if you were looking for some deep, intellectual philosophy or elaborate rituals requiring superhuman self-discipline to transform your life. Because you don't need them. All you need are habits. In fact, once you discover the power of habits, you will find that some of the simplest habits can have the biggest impact on your life.

I want to show you how by adopting five simple habits every morning, success can be within your reach. By changing a few simple things you do every day, you can transform your whole life. Again, I know it almost sounds too simple to work, but it isn't. However, because most people can't see it that way, they will stay where they are month after month, year after year, same job, same house, same haircut...

Personally, I was ecstatic when I found out that simple changes in my daily routine might have a dramatic impact on my life. Could doing some simple things like exercising or reading my goals each day really be the springboard I needed to launch myself into the life of my dreams? I was skeptical too.

But I had been doing my homework. I had read about how others had used this very formula of Five Powerful Habits to completely transform themselves: people like Tony Robbins, Warren Buffet, Margaret Thatcher, and John Maxwell, just to name a few. If it worked for them, I reasoned, it had to work for me too. And guess what? It will work for you, as well.

In this book, you'll find out just how a third generation welfare recipient went from rags to riches, transforming himself into a multimillionaire businessman just by changing what he did every morning. How a young mother transformed her marriage, career, and even her personality with five morning habits. How successful CEOs and entrepreneurs use these five habits to get them where they are and keep them there, all before most people even roll out of bed.

Incorporating these five things into your morning will transform your life. The level of transformation is up to you. Once you define what success is, you can reach it. These habits might seem small and almost insignificant, but don't let that fool you! They are extremely powerful catalysts in your search for success.

But first, you have to make the commitment that you will do them, every day, day in and day out. Robert Collier said, "Success is the sum of small efforts repeated day after day."

In each chapter, we will look at one of five different habits you can add to your morning routine to start you on the road to success. We'll discuss why these habits are the well-kept secret of some of the world's most successful people, as well as why tackling this before 8 a.m. is so transforming. Then, I'll show you how to easily make it a habit of your very own, including some specific suggestions you can quickly put into action today in the Take Action section you will find at the end of each chapter.

Make sure to take at least one of the suggestions in the Take Action section at the end of each chapter and then DO IT! Action is the key. So grab one of the actions recommended and start incorporating it into your morning routine. Start with just one of these habits and keep doing it every morning until it's routine, even if you're only getting up five minutes earlier to do 12 pushups. It's a start and it will get the ball rolling. Then add the next one.

For those of you who are naturally early risers, you may be able to incorporate several, or even all of these habits from the start. There is no need to wake up two hours earlier than usual to fit these five things into your morning. You could dedicate just five minutes to each habit and still see amazing results. No matter what your morning routine looks like right now, you can begin to incorporate better habits into your morning. Start where you're at and keep going!

And if you are definitely not an early riser, don't despair! While I want to encourage you to start your morning with a success routine, how you define "morning" isn't so much the point as just setting aside time to focus on your success before your day gets going. Perhaps you are a night shift worker and your "morning" begins at 8 p.m. rather than 8 a.m. Perhaps you have a baby at home who dictates when your morning starts. You can still put these five habits into practice and see results, even if it doesn't happen by 8 a.m. I'll even give you some examples of how others have made it work for them.

To help you implement these five simple habits into your morning routine, I created a downloadable workbook that you can simply print off to record your thoughts and help you take action. I want to stress again that it's only the things you DO that will change your life! So grab your workbook at the link below and let's get started transforming your life!

Download the workbook at:

www.overcomingauto/mydworkbook

CHAPTER 1
SUCCESS IS FOUND IN YOUR DAILY ROUTINE

Personal development and leadership expert John Maxwell is famously quoted as saying, "You'll never change your life until you change something you do daily. The secret of your success is found in your daily routine." In this book, we'll delve into exactly how to change your daily routine from one of just going through the motions to one that sets you up for unlimited success. You'll read countless examples of people who started out as your average Joe and who turned their lives around to experience unprecedented success simply by changing their habits.

But before we get into those five life-changing habits, let's first talk about what success is. Or, more specifically, what it is for *you*. You might have picked up this book because you were drawn to the idea of being successful: of having more, being more, and doing more. But before you can have/be/do more, you need to define what that is for you. It's great to read about the stellar successes of famous businessmen millionaires, but if you can't see yourself as that successful, chances are you won't get there. And maybe "there" isn't really where you want to be, anyway.

Jack Canfield once said, "One of the main reasons why most people don't get what they want, is they haven't decided what they want. They haven't defined their desires in clear and compelling detail." As the author of the famous *Chicken Soup for the Soul* book series, he certainly knows what he's talking about. Canfield's publisher laughed at him when he told them of his goal to sell 1.5 million copies of the book by December 30, 1994. They weren't laughing, however, when *Chicken Soup for the Soul* exceeded that goal, selling over 8 million copies worldwide. That's the power of knowing what you really want!

Earl Nightengale, respected author, speaker, and the Dean of Personal Development, defined success as the progressive realization of a worthy ideal. Maybe your worthy ideal is to grow your business to over $1 million annually. Maybe it's to raise your children to be kind, considerate, and servant-hearted, or to build a homeless shelter in your community. Whatever your worthy ideal is, make sure you acknowledge it, embrace it, and make it fully yours.

In other words, don't try to make someone else's definition of success your own. Otherwise, you will be miserable in pursuit of a goal that doesn't have your heart and your passion. I found this to be true a few years ago when my children were very young and I left the workforce to stay home to care for them. Many of the other moms I knew were hotly pursuing corporate success in the workplace. There's nothing wrong with that, but I knew that it wasn't what I was supposed to be doing. My heart was in cultivating a strong, healthy relationship with my children and setting them on their own course to successful adulthood.

Occasionally, though, I would mentally compare myself to those other moms, feeling inferior because I wasn't making the big bucks they were. Do you think I would have felt satisfied showing up to work every day just to say I earned that paycheck when that's not where my heart was?

Now that my kids are a little older, my priorities have changed again. I still hold my relationship with my kids as one of the most important pieces of my life, but I have more time to focus on my passions and interests, and time to grow my business now that they are in school.

Before you can begin the process of creating a successful routine, take the time to define why you are doing it. Otherwise, it's just motion and busy-ness, and the first time the going gets a little tough (hello, 6 a.m. alarm clock on a cold January morning!) you'll be tempted to hit snooze, pull the covers over your head, and say forget it!

Define What Success Is for *You*

I want you to take some time to define what success is for you. What do you want to have? To be? To do? Allow yourself to dream. Ask yourself what your interests and passions are.

Write it down, and don't censor yourself because you think your vision of success is too big or too crazy to come true. Don't rush through this process. Take at least 15 minutes to write down your vision for the future. You can always add to it later.

In your workbook, record your insights as you read through Make Your Day. This is part of the "taking action" phase of implementing changes in your routine. So don't just read each chapter, think, “Hmmm, that was interesting,” and then promptly forget about it. Positive results only come about because of positive action!

Why 5 Things?

Now that you’ve defined what success is for you, I want to totally change your definition of success again! You’ve gotten clear on your vision, and what you want out of life. That’s the first step in achieving success. But there is another side to success that is just as important.

In fact, if you overlook this piece of the puzzle, your beautiful dream of success will likely fall flat on its face. Remember how John Maxwell said that the secret to your success is found in your daily routine? ... Read it again...... Read it again.... Do you see it? *Success is*. Success is found in your daily routine. Don’t think of success as the big dream you wrote down: the award, the sports car, the huge bank account.

Think of success as conquering your daily routine.

So many people have high hopes for their future but they get bogged down in the details. Their dream seems too big, too impossible, too improbable. When you wrote down your vision for a successful life, maybe you thought that too. Maybe you thought that you would love to write that book, start that company, own that dream house. But your mind did this thing where it kind of went off the rails and a little voice told you that it was probably not going to happen.

That's because you're focusing on the wrong thing. Oh, this is so beautiful, I hope you can see it! In fact, it's called the *secret* to success because most people can't. But I'm trusting that you are going to open your eyes to the simplicity of success: your daily habits.

Success isn't the big awards, the promotion, the full bank account, the book deal, or even the happy marriage. Success is conquering your daily routine. Most people miss it because, frankly, it's so mundane. We want success to be the certificates, the awards, the recognition. The big stuff. And it is. But first, it's the small stuff. Reading your goals every day. (If you haven't tried this, trust me: after about the 256th day, it might get a little boring. Do it anyway.) Exercising. Reading. Every. Day.

Study the lives of successful people and you'll find that they've mastered their daily routine. They're intentional about how they spend their time. John Maxwell once wrote in an article for success.com that he gets a chuckle when people tell him they wish they could spend a day with him. Why? Because, according to Maxwell, his days are pretty dull.

Most of his days don't reflect the high-powered, exciting life of a successful entrepreneur. Rather, Maxwell insists, his days are routines that probably aren't the makings of the next mega-blockbuster movie. It's mastering those routines, those daily habits, if you will, that make the exciting moments possible. Speaking in front of crowds of thousands doesn't just happen. You prepare for it.

As a matter of fact, Maxwell practically coined the idea of cultivating five daily habits intended to

achieve success. Maxwell defines his Rule of 5 as a series of activities one does every day that are fundamental to success. Every day Maxwell does five things: he reads, he files, he thinks, he asks questions, and he writes. And he's not the only one.

Cynthia Pasquella, celebrity nutrition coach and creator of the Institute of Transformational Nutrition, also maximizes her morning hours with a routine aimed towards success. In fact, Cynthia credits her daily routines to keeping her on top of her game. Cynthia tells the online magazine *Divine Living* that she starts every morning with journaling, including three things she's grateful for, her three daily intentions, and free form journaling. She follows that up with 20 minutes of meditation and some stretching. This routine helps keep her grounded and peaceful rather than starting the day off in a rush.

It’s been said that you will never experience victory in public until you first find victory in private. Gain the mastery of your daily routine and you will truly be the master of your destiny. The five things we are about to discuss are some of the simplest habits around. For the most part, they probably aren't new or unusual to you.

But what you might have missed in these daily habits is the amazing power they inherently hold to radically transform your life. If you learn to look at these five habits with the eyes of a successful person rather than viewing them as mundane, you will be harnessing an incredible transformative power. And I promise you this: you will never be the same.

CHAPTER 2
SECRETS OF HABIT FORMATION

Our five simple things *will* change your life. But only if they become habit. What is a habit, anyway, and what makes habits such powerful catalysts of change?

Habits are defined as a routine of behavior that tends to occur unconsciously. Because they occur unconsciously, habits can have a very powerful effect on the direction of your life.

Brushing your teeth is often held up as a classic example of how habit formation works. Assuming you do brush your teeth, you probably do it every morning without even thinking about it. Same time. Same place. Chances are, you're even thinking about other things while you're doing it: what you're going to wear today or if you can catch that shoe sale after work before your kids' basketball practice.

You likely don't give much thought to brushing your teeth anymore. But think about how significant this habit is. Imagine what would happen if you dropped the habit of brushing your teeth and never did it again. Besides having yucky, fuzzy teeth you would be sure to notice after a few days, what would happen to your teeth after a few years?

Very likely, tooth decay and gum disease would set in. You might find yourself sporting a nice pair of dentures in your later years (or earlier years!). Did you know that research also links dental problems with other health problems such as heart disease and autoimmune diseases? Could the simple habit of brushing your teeth keep a heart attack at bay in your later years? Maybe even save your life? Bet you didn't realize how much was riding on that daily 60-second ritual, huh?

Habits are like the slow drip of water, faithfully cutting into the rock, day after day. It's so slow that at first it seems completely insignificant. Come back in a year, however, and you can see the small indentation the water has made. In a few years, the path is wider. Over time, it has cut a course the size of a river through the mountain.

We understand how action compounded over time is all it takes for something as small as a drop of water to become a mighty river that cuts huge mountains into vast canyons. Habits are those small, seemingly insignificant actions, that, when compounded daily, have the ability to make sweeping changes in one's life. Remember John Maxwell's admonition that your life will never change until you change something you do daily? Those things you do daily are simply your *habits* that set the course for your life.

It all boils down to automating the actions that will bring about the desired results. Research into habit formation tells us exactly how to do that. In the book *The Power of Habit*, Charles

Duhigg outlines the latest research into habit formation. Simply put, there first must be a cue, and then a clearly defined reward.

A cue, or, as I like to call it, a trigger, is a call to action. It's the little bell dinging that makes the dog start salivating. And this is where setting up your five daily habits in the a.m. makes it simple to create triggers. Your trigger can simply be the sound of your alarm clock going off. It can be rolling out of bed and seeing your workout clothes laying on the dresser – they're your trigger to start exercising! Having a bowl of fresh fruit already cut up and sitting front and center on the refrigerator shelf will be your trigger to eat a healthy breakfast.

In each chapter, as we discuss how to make your five habits part of your morning, we'll discuss some easy triggers you can use to make sure you are setting yourself up to be successful at your routine to, well, be successful. Before we move on to the second part of habit formation, rewards, let's drill down into creating strong triggers that will ensure strong habits.

Setting Up Habit Triggers

As I said before, the key to making your new morning routine stick is automating it. Let me give you a perfect example of how to automate your routine from pro blogger Ruth Soukup. When Ruth wanted to create a morning routine that maximized her productive time, she made a list of the habits she wanted to be a part of her morning. Next, she explains in her book *Living Well, Spending Less*, she wrote down every step, from getting dressed to having coffee, prayer time, etc. She goes on to explain that she made her list out in detail so she would be able to do it in the same order every morning until those actions became an ingrained habit.

This is one great way to automate your morning routine. After reading this suggestion in Ruth's book, I tried it with my own morning routine and now it's so automatic I could probably sleepwalk through it! While I was developing my morning habits I kept my routine list in the front of my planner where I could refer to it.

My morning routine steps looked like this:

- Wake up at 5:45 a.m.
- Read Positive Declarations
- Journal
- Read Goals– Long-Term, Monthly and Weekly goals
- Set Daily Goals and To Do List
- Read Bible/ Prayer
- Yoga
- Take Vitamins
- Shower
- Dress
- Breakfast

Creating a morning routine that you complete in the same order every day will help you quickly establish good morning habits rather than spending a lot of mental real estate wondering what you should do next. In fact, the more time you spend making decisions, the quicker your mind will run out of mental energy that you could be using on other things. Experts call this phenomenon Decision Making Fatigue. We'll look at Decision Making Fatigue in the next chapter, but suffice it to say for now that it's something you want to avoid at all costs if you want to remain productive throughout your day.

By the way, if my list looks long, keep in mind that most of these tasks only take a few minutes to complete. It only takes me about an hour from start to finish, including showering, dressing and eating breakfast! You don't need to spend hours journaling, for example. Even two minutes of journaling, doing 10 pushups, or jotting a quick list of daily goals will go a long way in maximizing the quality of the rest of your day.

The amount of time you spend on your daily routine isn't the point. In fact, if waking up early sounds like the makings of your worst nightmare (*morningmare?*), then start small. Set your alarm clock for five minutes earlier than you normally wake up. You could spend literally one minute on each habit, with the exception of eating a healthy breakfast. I definitely recommend taking your time with that one!

As you adjust to your new routine, you can adjust the time you wake up, if needed. In fact, you may not need to adjust your waking time at all if you are able to make better use of the way you are already spending your morning!

So often, we have the mindset that if we can't devote a large amount of time to something, then it's not worth doing at all. Don't fall prey to this type of thinking. Small hinges swing big doors. The point isn't how much time you spend, it's that you are consistent. The biggest point is to just keep going.

Rewards: The Power of Joy and Celebration

In researching habit formation I came across another great little secret to make habits stick for the long haul that I want to share with you. Before I tell you what it is, you need to realize that habits are routines that help you get something positive or avoid something negative. Honing in on the "something positive" will keep your habits going strong. Specifically, I'm talking about the power of joy and celebration in setting up habits. Let me explain.

In *Surprisingly Unstuck,* author Maria Brilaki explains that celebration increases motivation. Sometimes our goals seem too big or take longer than we like, causing motivation to disappear faster than low-fat brownies at a Weight Watchers meeting. When we use rewards to keep us motivated, our brain begins to look for ways to keep the rewards coming.

So even if you made a small step toward developing your new habit, be sure to celebrate! Promise yourself you can read a chapter from that new novel on your nightstand before bed. Buy yourself that new gadget you've been eyeing once you reach your goal of writing for one hour each day for a month. Even just a mental high-five can go a long way in keeping you on track!

By the way, when I say small step, I really mean *small step*. If you set your alarm for five minutes earlier so you could start a rock star morning routine… but ended up hitting snooze and falling back to sleep...Celebrate! Yes, I'm serious. Celebrate that you remembered to set your alarm. It shows you were thinking about your goal of getting up earlier. You are moving in the right direction. "If you are serious about making a healthier living change, then you should be serious about celebrating. No exceptions," Maria writes.

Besides, beating yourself up over every little mistake will only serve to push you further from where you want to be. Our minds have this pesky little habit of rebelling at words like *have to* or *should*. Try saying this: "I get to get up and start my day off well so I can enjoy success all day long." Now compare that to "I should get up early and exercise." See? Looking at your morning routine as an opportunity rather than an obligation will make a radical difference in whether or not you are successful in sticking with it.

I hope I've convinced you that creating an amazing morning routine is completely doable and totally worth it. Take time to write down in the workbook what your morning habit routine will look like. There is also a place for you to record how you will celebrate and reward yourself. Be sure to include bigger rewards, like a nice purchase for hitting a big goal. Don't forget to include smaller rewards, like a quick happy dance in the kitchen after you eat a healthy breakfast.

CHAPTER 3
WHY THE A.M.?

We've already discussed how powerful morning habits can be in transforming your life. But maybe you're still thinking, "Why the morning? Why can't I just do these habits anytime?" And the short answer is, you can. However, I hope you will give me a chance to convince you that getting off on the right foot each day just may be the best way to fast forward your success. Let's explore four reasons why an a.m. routine is the way to go.

A Morning Routine Sets the Tone for the Day

Rolling out of bed after hitting the snooze button a few times and then shoving in a few mouthfuls of cereal while screaming at your kids to get their shoes on is no way to start the day. Unfortunately, the negative tone you begin the day with can follow you around all day long.

Why not set yourself up for some positive energy throughout the day instead? Try taking the time to start your day intentionally, to nourish your spirit, soul, and body through our five things, and see if your entire day doesn't turn out better, as well. Once our five things become habit, you will find yourself enjoying your morning ritual, and you'll be reaping the benefits all day long.

Our actions tend to have a ripple effect that radiate throughout the rest of the day. Not only that, but they can also affect others around us. Try rushing your kids out the door and see if your grumpy attitude doesn't rub off on them. Or notice how your co-workers respond to your exasperated and disheveled appearance next time you show up late to work. You might just be surprised at how something as simple as a relaxed morning routine can affect something as seemingly unrelated as how others see you and treat you.

Distractions Tend to Be Minimized in the Morning

Nothing like getting home from a long, brutal day at the office to a long list of To Do's: walk the dog, make dinner, give the kids a bath and whoops! — your best intentions to work out have gotten waylaid by the demands of everyday life. Making time for your top priorities *before* the day gets crowded with other, often less important activities (I'm looking at you, social media) is the best way to ensure that they actually get done.

I'm not taking any excuses from night owls here, either. If you tend to do your best work later in the day, great! As you spend a few minutes *each morning* on our five things, you can be sure to pencil in time to do your most important stuff when you're at your best, whether that's 8 am or 8 pm. Having set a good tone for the day by practicing our five things in the morning, you'll be able to achieve everything on your daily To Do list while still maintaining your good vibes.

Your Focus and Energy Tend to be Highest in the Morning

Speaking of that long list of distractions – er, I mean To Do's – I'm sure you've noticed how your mental energy tends to be zapped after too many tasks. Research has shown that while our brains are pretty darn awesome, they tend to be subject to something called Decision Making Fatigue.

Decision Making Fatigue (can we just call it DMF?) is just what it sounds like. When we have too many decisions to make, our brains get overwhelmed to the point where we just can't seem to make any more decisions; at least not good ones, anyway. Instead, we tend to revert to emotions and snap judgements to make our decisions for us, something that tends to not serve us well in the long run.

A study published in 2011 by the National Academy of Sciences demonstrates just how dangerous DMF can be. In this study, researchers examined the rulings of parole board judges and found that parolees would receive favorable outcomes on their cases earliest in the day, with a favorable outcome being handed out in about 65% of cases.

As the morning wore on, however, and Decision Making Fatigue set in, favorable rulings would dwindle, dropping off to zero! After a nice lunch break, when the judges would apparently refresh themselves mentally and physically, favorable outcomes would bounce back up (but dwindle back down to zero again as the day wore on).

This study isn't just interesting to know in case you find yourself on the wrong side of the law and facing a parole board one day. It illustrates how Decision Making Fatigue can prevent you from making good decisions, no matter how noble your intentions are.

Setting up your morning routine can keep Decision Making Fatigue at bay, not only when it comes to deciding when/where/how to follow through with your five things, but it can also keep DMF in 'off mode' all day long. When you've set up a morning routine that includes planning your day, you end up making your biggest decisions first thing, before DMF has a chance to rear its ugly head.

By the time your brain has puttered out of decision-making energy, your biggest decisions have already been made. You already penciled into your planner what you were making for dinner so you won't need to reach for the cereal box at 6 p.m because you're too tired to think about whipping up something healthy and delicious. You've already made an appointment with your personal trainer after work, so no need to make the overwhelming decision of when and how to work out. Just show up and go through your training routine!

A Morning Routine Is a Reflection of How You See Yourself

I hate to get all touchy-feely with you since we just met, but the fact of the matter is, the way you spend your morning is as much a reflection of your self-worth as the results of that quiz on loving yourself you found in *Cosmopolitan*. If you see yourself as a success in the making, you'll make the effort to put your best self forward each day.

If you wake up late every morning, however, piddling away your precious morning hours by getting caught up in the latest gossip talk show on the television, or fighting with your spouse over whose turn it is to use the bathroom, you might want to ask yourself a few tough questions.

Do you really feel that you deserve to be successful? That you're worth it? If you can honestly answer yes to those questions, great! Then make the time to do what successful people do and you'll soon find yourself hitting goal after goal as you climb the ladder to success.

If you can't honestly answer yes to those questions, however, then it's time to take a good look in the mirror, get straight with yourself, and proclaim that you *are* successful. From now on, you're not going to sabotage your own efforts at self-improvement. Even if you don't feel it yet, set yourself up on a morning routine that moves you in the direction you want to go. Before long, your strides in the right direction will be the momentum you need to keep up the positive actions you are creating each day.

Think of those positive actions as oars propelling your ship to its intended destination.

If you'll allow me a corny illustration, your map is the vision you created back in chapter one. It's the inner picture you have inside of where you want to go. Our five things are the vehicle to get you there. As you move your ship through the waters, the oars of daily action move you closer to the destination: Success.

By the way, I hope you notice that I'm not telling you what "a.m." means to you. For some, it could mean waking up at 5 a.m., or earlier (yikes!). Some people thrive on early mornings.

If that's not you, don't fret. Waking up at 8 a.m. or even a little later can still be wildly productive as long as that means you are giving yourself the time to get up and go through some simple habits without rushing around like a madman, or falling behind on your tasks that need to get done (like say, getting to work on time or getting your kids up and out the door so they don't miss the bus). You can make these habits yours in a way that truly *is* yours. The point is to *make* them.

As you can see, mornings rock. So take the time to let our five things ground and focus you as you start each day so that you can give your best to whatever lies ahead. As we discuss each of the five habits, we'll get a little more specific about why completing each of the five things is best done in the morning, and how to use these habits to maximize your morning routine. For now, let's dive right into our five things!

CHAPTER 4
SUCCESSFUL PEOPLE REVIEW THEIR GOALS

While goal setting isn't a foreign concept to most people, *goal getting* unfortunately is. Have you ever made a New Year's resolution? Most people do. Yet statistics show that only 8% of those who set New Year's resolutions actually achieve them. Only 8%! The key to seeing your goals become a reality is to not just make goals, but to *keep them in front of you*. Every day.

Most people miss this key when setting goals. They may take the time to write out their goals, perhaps even going so far as to make them specific and measurable. Then they stick them in a drawer and never look at them again. In this chapter I'll show you why successful people know better than to make that mistake, and how reviewing your goals daily will monumentally increase your chances of actually achieving them. Plus, I've got some fun and creative tips for keeping your goals front and center!

Why Successful People Review Their Goals Daily

In 1996 Bruce Jenner addressed a group of Olympic hopefuls. “How many of you have your goals written down?” he asked these high performance athletes. Not surprisingly, every hand was raised. Next he asked, “How many of you have your goals with you now?” Only one hand went up. That hand belonged to Dan O’Brien, who went on to win the Olympic Decathlon in the 1996 Olympics.

Without a doubt, having goals is paramount to achieving success. Professional speaker and goal-setting expert Brian Tracy calls the ability to set goals and make plans for their accomplishment the “master skill” of success. Why are goals such an integral part of achieving success? Because goals are your roadmap to doing great things. Without a roadmap, you’ll end up lost every time.

When I was in middle school, we had different modules every few weeks in gym class where we got to try new sports and athletic endeavors. In one module, we learned archery. If you've never tried it, there's nothing more satisfying than aiming your arrow, pulling it back, and hitting the target right in the bullseye. And nothing is more disappointing than completely missing the target and watching your arrow go sailing off into a grassy field so you can spend the next 20 minutes searching for it.

It does, however, make a great lesson on life in general. Motivational speaker Zig Ziglar said, "If you aim at nothing, you'll hit it every time." Imagine closing your eyes, pulling back, and shooting your arrow in any direction without taking the time to line up your sights and aim. How many times do you think you'd hit the bullseye, or even the target, for that matter? Of course, that sounds like a ridiculous way to practice archery, yet it's exactly how many people approach their lives. Goals are your

"Ready, Aim, Fire" in the game of life. Trust me when I say nothing is more satisfying than hitting your goals every time.

Why Before 8 a.m.?

Bill Gates and Warren Buffett were having dinner together one evening when they were asked what they thought was the single most important factor in their success. Reportedly, they both answered, "Focus." Knowing what you want and then taking the steps to bring it about is the essence of focus. When your goals are clearly defined, you know what you really want from life. In other words, you're focused.

Reading your goals every morning upgrades your focus to laser-like precision. When you start your day reminding your subconscious mind of what you really want from life, your brain goes to work to make it happen. Reviewing your goals allows you to prioritize your tasks for the day.

If your goal is to write a book this year, for example, reminding yourself of your goal everyday makes it much harder to put it off and forget about it! From your written goals, you can map out your day to make sure you prioritize what's really important rather than wasting time putting out fires and mindlessly scrolling through social media. Is one of your goals to improve your marriage? Pencil in a 20 minute pow-wow with your sweetie before dinner, or schedule a date night for next Friday. Trying to drop a few pounds? Write that power walk with your bestie into your planner right now so it doesn't get overlooked.

I keep my yearly goals written in the front of my daily planner so it's easy to read through them each morning and then transfer those goals into my weekly and daily tasks. Over the last year I enrolled in a health coaching program to help me achieve a lifelong goal of helping others transform their lives through nutrition and lifestyle choices.

Since this was a self-paced course, there was no one there to check up on whether or not I was sticking to my goal of completing the course on time. I made sure to schedule time into my planner each week to complete my coursework rather than allowing other, less important issues to cause me to fall behind. I'm happy to report that as of the publishing date of this book, I finished my course ahead of schedule and am all set up to help others transform their lives through the power of nutrition. Bullseye!

Making It a Habit

If you don't already have written goals in place, let's talk about how to set a good goal. Remember back in chapter one, when we defined success by creating a vision of what a successful life meant to you? Goals take that vision and break it down into actionable steps to make it a reality.

Many people set goals that are too vague: "lose weight" or "save money" or "have a better marriage," for example. These are great things to aspire to, but they are so vague, how will you know if you reach them? "Save money" could mean you saved $5,000 this year… or it could mean you saved $20.

Your goals should include two criteria: how much and by when. How much money do you want to save? How much weight do you want to lose? Once you decide how much, the next step is to decide when you want to achieve this goal. "I will save $3000 by December 31st" is much more clear and actionable than "I want to save money." Once you're clear on how much and by when, it's easy to break your goal down into smaller action steps.

Let's say your vision for the future includes owning your own home debt-free. Perhaps that feels like a totally unrealistic goal, but once you begin to break it down into smaller goals, you'll soon realize that it is totally possible! And once you begin to see your dream as a possibility, you'll begin to take action to move towards it.

Since your goal is to have a debt-free home, you may make a goal to add an extra $200 onto your house payment each month to pay down the principle. As you begin to see progress on your goal, your excitement will begin to build. Use that momentum to keep moving forward. You may begin brainstorming ideas to bring in extra income, or you may decide to put your tax refund toward the goal instead of blowing it all on things you didn't really need, anyway.

I know I've already said it, but I'm going to say it again. Whatever goals you decide on, make sure to put them in writing! For one thing, writing your goals down shows that you're serious about accomplishing them. Not only that, but it will also give you clarity on what you really want and what you need to do. Let's go back to your goal to save $3000 this year. This goal is specific and measurable: a certain amount within a certain time frame. Now break it down into even smaller goals. Saving $3000 in 12 months equates to $250 a month. You might have some months where you are able to put aside a little more towards your goals, but having your goal broken down this way will help you to see if you are moving in the right direction.

Take Action! Suggestions for Goal Setting

Goal setting can truly change your life! Let me give you a few suggestions that can make reaching your goals even easier.

- **Find an accountability partner** to keep you on track with your goals. There's nothing like sharing your goals with someone else to keep you on track! Just make sure you choose someone who believes in you and who encourages you to move forward, especially during those times when you might fall behind.

- **Writing your top 3 goals out every day for 30 days** is a great way to supercharge your momentum! Just spend a few minutes each day for 30 days writing out your top goals and see if it doesn't make a huge difference in how fast you reach them.

- **A vision board** is a great way to keep your goals in front of you, as well! This can be as simple or as complex as you want, but be sure to place images of what you are striving towards: a picture of the check filled in with the amount you want to see on your paycheck, or a photo of the new vehicle you've been drooling over. Our minds tend to think in images so adding pictures to your goals helps you grab hold of your vision and make it a reality. I like to include inspiring quotes and sayings on my vision board, too.

Goal setting may just be one of the most powerful transformative practices you incorporate into your life. Just don't forget our top success secret: *keep those goals in front of you*! As you look at your goals every day, you will find yourself moving towards them as amazing opportunities present themselves and doors begin to open for you to step into the life of your dreams!

In your workbook, write down three to five goals you want to accomplish in the next 12 months. Make sure they are in line with your vision of success. If your vision is to be debt free then paying off your credit cards might be a better goal for this year than going on a dream vacation. Save the dream vacation as a reward for paying off those debts and you'll enjoy relaxing on the beach in Mexico much more when you know you won't be paying for it long after it's over.

CHAPTER 5
VISUALIZE YOUR FUTURE

It's no secret among the successful set that what you focus on, you become. In this chapter you'll see how some of the world's most successful people use visualization to get to the top of their game. Then we'll look at how to make it a simple habit in your success routine so you can see the same results! I've got some great ideas to share with you on making this habit easy and doable.

Why Successful People Visualize Their Future

The late, great Dr. Norman Vincent Peale was well known for encouraging audiences to improve their lives through the power of positive thinking. I mean, the guy wrote the book on it! But even Dr. Peale knew that positive thinking alone was not enough to create success. In his book, *Positive Imaging*, he explains that visualization is taking positive thinking one step further. "Imaging, the forming of mental pictures or images, is based on the principle that there is a deep tendency in human nature to ultimately become precisely like that which we imagine or image ourselves as being," he writes.

Research into visualization is bearing out what self-help gurus already knew. We do indeed become what we think about. Visualization stimulates the same areas of the brain that are activated when we perform the action we are imagining, without even moving a muscle. In 2004, researchers reported in the *Journal of Neuropsychologia* that study participants were able to increase muscle strength by mentally performing exercises to nearly the same degree as those who actually executed the motions physically.

Sports psychologists love to use the technique of visualization to help professional athletes stay on their A game. Professional golfer Jack Nicklaus, who won over 100 tournament victories in his esteemed career, once said, "I never hit a shot, not even in practice, without having a very sharp, in-focus picture of it in my head." He goes on to describe his technique of visualizing the shot by "seeing" the trajectory of the ball and its perfect landing on the green right where he wants it, including the type of swing that makes that perfect landing a reality.

In 2011, after winning the U.S. Open against then #1-seeded Roger Federer and rising to the top spot in tennis, Novak Djokovic told a reporter for the *New York Times* how visualization was an integral part of his success on the court. "One of the ways is to kind of meditate but not meditate with the intention of going away from those problems, but visualize. Visualization is a big part of everybody's life, not just athletes. I strongly believe in visualization. I believe that there is a law of attraction: You get the things that you produce in your thoughts. Life just works that way," he said. Djokovic must have been a champion at visualization as well as tennis! He used the mental technique of visualization to get to the top of his game and stay there, going down in history as one of the top tennis players of all time.

Visualization is a success habit that works for more than just athletic endeavors, as well! Take for instance, the story of Natan Sharansky, who spent 9 years imprisoned in the USSR after being accused of spying for the US. Not one to let the grass grow under his feet, Sharansky put the time to good use, playing himself in mental chess while locked in solitary confinement and telling himself, "I might as well use the opportunity to become the world champion!" After his release from prison, Sharansky did indeed become the world champion when he defeated reigning champion Garry Kasparov in 1996.

You may have heard the now famous story of Jim Carrey's overwhelming success as a Hollywood actor. Years before anyone knew him as anything more than a struggling stand-up comedian, Carrey would drive his old pick-up truck to the top of Mulholland Drive, look out over the city, and imagine his future. In an interview with Oprah Winfrey in 1997, Carey went on to explain that he wrote out a check to himself for $10 million "for acting services rendered." He dated the check for Thanksgiving of 1995 and carried it in his wallet for years. Amazingly, just before Thanksgiving in 1995, he learned that he was indeed set to make $10 million for the movie *Dumb and Dumber*.

Countless examples abound of ordinary people who visualized themselves as overwhelming successful, and who then went on to turn that image into reality. If you're serious about seeing your vision of a successful life become a reality for you, don't leave this awesome weapon of self-mastery laying on the table. Let's make it a habit!

Making It a Habit

Remember, when we do something at the same time and in the same place each day, it solidifies the habit formation. We've already talked about reading your goals each day and why doing so first thing every day will help you set your intentions and To Do's. Visualization will take the process of reaching your goals even further, so I suggest adding it to your morning routine right after you review your goals, or even *while* you review your goals. As you read each goal, take a moment to close your eyes and imagine the goal as already being accomplished.

In his book *The Success Principles*, Jack Canfield suggests kicking your visualization process up a notch by adding all five senses to the imagination. If your goal is to take a 10-year anniversary trip to Italy, don't just picture stepping off the plane and onto Italian soil. Imagine how fresh the pasta will taste, how sweet the gelato will be. Imagine the sound of the pole moving through the water and the gondoliers shouting to one another as you drift lazily through the streets of Venice with your sweetheart.

And most of all, Canfield writes, imagine the intense emotions you'll feel when you have the experience. Research has proved that when a scenario is associated with intense emotion, it has a powerful effect on memory. So be sure to imagine the excitement you'll feel at seeing the Pieta, the satisfaction of polishing off that fettucine alfredo, and the love and joy you will share with your lover while strolling hand in hand down an Italian boulevard.

Visualizing your goals each morning is like putting rocket fuel in your gas tank; you will get to where you want to be much faster when you take the time to envision your goals as already completed. The following suggestions will help you get started designing a visualization program that works for you.

Take Action! Suggestions for Visualizing Your Future

- **Use images** to enhance the visualization process. If you created a vision board with images that represent the realization of your dreams and goals, this is the time to use them! Want to lose weight? Put up a photo of a fit person, or a photo of yourself when you were your ideal weight. If your goal is to have a certain amount of money in your savings account, make up a savings statement with your goal amount printed on the balance line. Then use these pictures during the visualization process to burn the image of success indelibly in your mind.

- **Take the time to write out a visualization** for each goal you have set for yourself. Take your goal of honeymooning in the Caribbean and write out how you will feel when you are experiencing the trip: what you will see, hear, do, etc. Read it out loud and then close your eyes and imagine yourself as actually experiencing what you wrote.

- **Create your own guided imagery** by recording yourself as you walk through the realization of your goals. Guided imagery is a specific type of visualization where you use a recording that leads you through a specific process to achieve a desired outcome. You can find pre-recorded guided imagery or make your own.

- **Visualization** can also include the idea of meditating on a thought or scripture in order to embed it into the subconscious mind. For example, take a scripture such as, "In all these things we are more than conquerors through him that loved us." (Romans 8:37). Read the scripture out loud, repeating it several times, thinking about it and internalizing the meaning. You will be acting like more than a conqueror in no time!

- **Five to ten minutes is plenty of time** to spend each day visualizing your goals. Simply take a few minutes to visualize each goal as already completed, internalizing sights, sounds, and feelings that go along with their accomplishment. Then go about your day! Your mind will get busy looking for ways to make your vision a reality!

CHAPTER 6
READ FROM A GOOD BOOK

There's a good reason why reading to children is a top recommendation from pediatricians to parents. The growth in language development, logic, and communication that reading fosters is evident to any parent who takes the time to read to their kiddos. And the benefits of reading don't end just because you outgrow PB&J. In this chapter, we'll look at some amazing transformations in the lives of those who made reading a top priority each day. Of course, I've got some great tips and tricks to make reading one of your top success habits, as well.

Why Successful People Read Daily

Want to know how one man went from a third generation welfare recipient, deeply in debt and working seven days a week, to a highly sought-after life coach and multimillionaire businessman? Peter Daniels grew up with all the tides turned against him, suffering from dyslexia and poor health as well as poverty that had been deeply entrenched for generations in his family tree.

As if all those strikes against him weren't enough, the cruel words of a grade-school teacher further solidified Daniels' self-image as a loser. When Peter Daniels was in the 3rd grade, his teacher called him to the front of the class and told him, "You're a bad boy, Peter Daniels, and you'll never amount to anything!"

Peter lived up to those words for many years. But when Daniels was 26 years old, something changed. After attending a Billy Graham Crusade in South Australia, Peter decided to turn things around. He bought three dictionaries to grow his vocabulary, as well as books on economics, politics, history, philosophy, and business.

Things didn't change immediately for Peter Daniels. He went into business three times, failing each time before he hit paydirt in real estate. He later went on to found the World Centre for Entrepreneurial Studies, making it his life goal to give away as much money as he could. Daniels boasts that he has read more than 5,000 biographies in his lifetime! Now that's a man who understands the power of the page!

This may just be the one morning habit that completely turns YOUR life around. In fact, some success coaches call reading the shortcut to success. Why? Because many successful people know that the company you keep determines your level of success.

And the easiest way to hang around the uber successful? Read their books. You can develop a mentor relationship with some of the top leaders in the business world just for the price of buying their book. Heck, you can do it for free if you use the library, although you are definitely going to want to spend at least a few hard-earned dollars on building a library of your own.

Take the books of those you admire most and make them your textbooks. Write in them. Highlight. Underline. Absorb them. They have the power to transform you.

In *The Slight Edge*, Jeff Olson declares continuous learning to be the most important force you can harness to accelerate and amplify your path through life. Unfortunately, most people never harness this force to propel them forward. Olson proves this point by sharing the following statistic: 58 percent of high school graduates who don't go on to college never read a book again for the rest of their lives! You'll probably never have an easier opportunity for personal and professional growth and mentorship than cracking open a good book for even a few minutes a day. Make sure you don't pass it by!

Why Before 8 a.m.?

Picture this. You're in college and it's 9:30 p.m. on a Tuesday night. That big final in your genetics class is tomorrow and you're studying one last time when you suddenly realize you've been reading mindlessly for the last 20 minutes and have no idea what you just read. Your brain has spent all day absorbing new information and now it's decided to take a little mini vacation to the student lounge, without your body. Sound familiar?

You already know most successful people prioritize their most important tasks by tackling them at the beginning of the day. Reading takes focus, and your mind is definitely freshest after a good night's sleep. You'll also be ready to implement your newfound knowledge right away as you tackle your problems for the day. No use giving yourself a slap on the forehead because you spent all day struggling with a problem, only to pick up a book with the solution right there in front of you after the fact.

Jim Rohn, author of more than 40 books on personal development, once stated, "What a man reads pours massive ingredients into his mental factory. Every day you need to stand guard to the door of your mind." The awesomeness quotient of your mental factory is only going to skyrocket when you make reading a morning habit.

Making It a Habit

Set a specific time every morning to read. Right after reading your goals and visualizing would be a great time. Choose your book and have it ready ahead of time so you aren't wasting precious minutes trying to decide what to read. (Take that, Decision Making Fatigue!)

You can read things besides books, by the way. Every morning, billionaire investor Warren Buffett reads multiple newspapers and financial reports as well as books. In fact, when Buffett began his career, he would read from 600 to 1000 pages a day. He still claims to spend about 80% of his day reading. "Look, my job is essentially corralling more and more and more facts and information and seeing whether that leads to some action," Buffett once told an interviewer.

Author and Personal Development guru Michael Hyatt claims that he spends about two hours a day reading, at least half of that in the a.m. Scrolling through his RSS feed every morning, he checks through the near 200 or so blogs he follows to read anything that catches his eye for the day. Hyatt rounds out his reading with the Bible and several newspapers like *The New York Times* and *Wall Street Journal*.

Take Action! Suggestions for Reading Daily

- **Read a variety of books.** Fiction. Poetry. Biographies. History. Don't just stick to business books, but learn as much as you can. Steve Jobs was reportedly obsessed with the works of poet William Blake. George Clooney claims *War and Peace* as his favorite read. He's the total package, with his GQ-worthy good looks and stunning intellect, isn't he?

- **Listen to audiobooks** while exercising. This is a great way to work your physical muscles and your mental muscles at the same time!

- **Make a reading list.** Choose 12 books that will challenge and inspire you and make a commitment to read them this year. That's just one book a month!

- **Join a book club** (or start one!) with a group of like-minded individuals. The bonus? You will have access to your own mastermind group to collaborate and bounce ideas off, as well as a way to keep each other accountable for putting all that knowledge into practice!

- **Make sure to build your library** as you go! Ebooks make books accessible for less than the price of the print version. Buying books used is another way to grow your collection.

- Here's a short list of some of my favorite books that will get you started on the path to success:
    - *The Slight Edge* by Jeff Olson
    - *The 7 Habits of Highly Effective People* by Stephen R Covey
    - *Think and Grow Rich* by Napoleon Hill
    - *Imagine Big* by Terri Savelle Foy

Now that you know what successful people know about the power of reading to transform you, don't wait to get started! Grab a great book and pencil in a few minutes each morning to expand your mind.

In your workbook, make a list of 12 books you want to read within the next year. Of course, these don't have to be the only books you read this year, but I encourage you to specifically choose 12 books that will stretch your thinking and encourage personal growth. As you read each book, I want to challenge you to write down in the workbook one take away that you will put into practice in your life and make your own. You will be well on your way to success, one page at a time!

CHAPTER 7
EAT A HEALTHY BREAKFAST

This habit may not sound that exciting, but it's actually one of my favorites! That's because I have learned to tap into the power of nutrition to keep me going strong and to help me be prepared to tackle anything that comes my way. Plus, I love to eat.

Let's have a little chat about why a healthy breakfast really will make you a champion. And if you need some help figuring out what a healthy breakfast actually is, I've got a few pointers for you there, as well.

Why Successful People Eat a Healthy Breakfast

I hate to sound like a public service announcement, but if you want to stay productive and going strong all day long, don't skip breakfast. Research shows that breakfast eaters maintain blood glucose levels over a 24-hour period better than those who skip the most important meal of the day. And that translates into the ability to maintain energy levels throughout the day without crashing. Your brain needs a steady supply of glucose to function at optimal levels. There is also a plethora of research that shows how eating breakfast leads to reduced stress levels, better concentration, and better emotional balance.

Not just any breakfast will do, though. Noshing on donuts and o.j. before dashing out the door will lead to blood sugar imbalances and a nasty spike in insulin and cortisol, your resident stress hormone. Studies have shown spikes in these hormones due to high sugar intake are linked to all kinds of mental woes, from poor concentration to Alzheimer's. Yikes!

In his book *The Adrenal Reset Diet*, Dr. Alan Christianson recommends a breakfast high in good-quality protein, alkalizing vegetables (think cabbage, broccoli, zucchini and such) as well as fiber and some healthy fats. This might mean rethinking what breakfast is for you. The easiest way to do this is just to think of breakfast as any other meal and not get locked into a "Breakfast has to be bagels and cereal" mindset. Once you get used to a nice warm bowl of chicken and veggie soup or a sausage and veggie stir-fry, you'll wonder why you ever thought toast was worthy of breaking your fast each morning.

Winston Churchill was a man who knew the power of a high-protein breakfast! Every morning he reportedly ate a large breakfast which consisted of a poached egg, toast, jam, grapefruit, cold meats...and a whiskey soda. Talk about eating hearty!

While I'm not sure whiskey sodas are the makings of a wholesome breakfast, choosing quality proteins and complex carbs can have a huge impact on how well you function throughout the day. Ziglar Inc. CEO Tom Ziglar discovered the power of a healthy breakfast several years ago. After his dad, beloved motivational speaker Zig Ziglar, passed away from the complications of a fall that led to a rapid decline in his health, Tom realized he needed to make some changes.

Watching his dad struggle with the beginning stages of memory loss after his fall, Tom had already learned that consuming gluten was associated with dementia and other health issues that come with aging. Not only that, Tom knew he could stand to lose a few pounds! So he put himself on a diet of whole, pure foods, eliminating processed foods and products made with refined flours and replacing them with fresh fruits, vegetables, legumes, nuts, and high-quality meats. Not only did Tom notice he began sleeping better, had more energy and got sick less, but he also dropped 66 pounds effortlessly!

Why Before 8 a.m.?

Dr. Christianson goes on to recommend eating within the first hour of waking, a habit I've found to be helpful in staying strong throughout the day. This is due, again, to those pesky hormones that like to control everything we do, from metabolism to emotions (hangry, anyone?).

Eating a healthy breakfast isn't just good for the hormones, though. Ever vowed to stick to your diet for the day, only to find yourself sneaking a cookie at 10 a.m.? Your next thought probably went something like this, "Well I just messed up so screw it! I'm having a triple bacon cheeseburger with a large order of fries and a milkshake for lunch!"

Setting yourself up with good habits earlier in the day tends to keep you on the straight and arrow later on. That's because good habits tend to snowball, making it easier to make good choices when you have stuck to your guns from the get-go. Nobody likes to break a winning streak! If you start your day with a healthy breakfast, chances are good you will find it much easier to stick to a healthy lunch, and then dinner.

Making It a Habit

Let's talk about how to change breakfast from just another mindless chore you go through each day (or not) to a powerful accelerator on your dash toward your dreams. As with all your morning habits, be sure to eat breakfast at the same time every day.

I've always been a breakfast eater, but sometimes I would get wrapped up in my morning rush and not eat breakfast until I was starving and irritable, and trust me, nobody wants that! Don't put off breakfast so that you have to shove a few mouthfuls of cornflakes in before sprinting out the door. Make a relaxed, energizing breakfast one of your top priorities.

If focusing on protein for breakfast sounds like a big change, make it easier for yourself by planning ahead. I write out my meal plan in my planner each week so I'm not standing in front of the fridge wondering what to do next. Many people plan to fail because they fail to plan.

Speaking of a high-protein breakfast, does giving up your morning donut habit sound like the makings of a bad break-up? Do yourself a favor and don't buy the donuts in the first place. If they aren't there, you can't eat them! I don't mean to insult your intelligence with this suggestion, but sometimes those bad habits are so ingrained we don't even realize what we're doing. If putting breakfast junk food in your grocery cart has become automatic, then this is your wake up call! Put the Frosted Flakes down and step away…

Finally, make it pleasurable. Eating is definitely meant to be a positive experience so make it something to look forward to. Play your favorite music while cooking and eating. Share your meal with people you enjoy spending time with (hopefully that's your family). Make breakfast a time to recharge and relax before facing your daily grind, and your mind and body will thank you for it!

Take Action! Suggestions for a Healthy Breakfast

Don't forget that protein is your friend in the a.m.! Try some of the following suggestions:

- Applegate Farms chicken sausage are delicious stir-fried with chopped veggies (broccoli, cabbage, zucchini, carrots – take your pick!)

- A quick soup may sound complicated to make in the morning, but it's really not. Just have all your veggies prepped the night before. Throw them in a pot with some chopped cooked chicken or other protein (fish is a great pick, too!) Add some broth and seasonings and let it simmer while you check off your other morning habits, like Reviewing Your

Goals. Sometimes multi-tasking can work!

- If you just can't give up the grains, or you are vegetarian, just make sure to pick a high-quality source, like steel-cut oats or gluten-free waffles topped with almond butter.

- Eggs can be a good source of protein in the morning, as well. A big ol' veggie omelet will definitely give you an edge!

- Full fat coconut milk or dairy milk yogurt with berries and a drizzle of honey can be a good choice in a pinch, but try to stick with higher protein breakfasts when you are able.

- Rely on leftovers whenever possible. What's easier than reheating that delicious meatball and butternut squash soup you made for dinner last night?

- Find a high-quality protein powder that is low in sugar. I like to mix mine with coconut milk to get the benefit of healthy fats. Almond milk can be another great choice.

- Speaking of healthy fats, don't forget to add them to the breakfast menu! Top your stir-fry or soup with a drizzle of olive oil or ghee, or add coconut oil to that oatmeal. You'll feel satisfied for much longer, not to mention that many important nutrients are fat-soluble and need to be consumed with some fat in order to be absorbed. Fat is your friend!

- I've given you a few ideas to chew on but regardless of what constitutes a healthy breakfast for you, be sure to make time to enjoy your meal, keeping it simple while still making a healthy choice. Your hormones and, consequently, your brain will thank you by returning the favor all day long!

Check out the workbook for a few of my favorite healthy recipes as well as some suggestions for where to find more info on healthy eating! Be sure to jot down a list of breakfast ideas you can pull from your workbook, as well, so when you're pinched for time you can consult your list and come up with a quick plan.

CHAPTER 8
MAKE TIME TO MOVE

Exercise. Just hearing the word can elicit feelings of dread and agony in many people. If that's you, then get ready for an attitude adjustment, stat! Allow me to convince you in this chapter that exercise is one of the most powerful habits successful people maintain – and why you'll want to maintain it, tool if you want to be numbered among the successful. Plus, I've got some helpful tips to easily make an a.m. exercise routine a habit that, dare I say it, you can actually enjoy! After all, we already know that if you don't enjoy it, your probably won't stick with it.

Why Successful People Exercise

I'm sure you know why exercise is such an important habit to maintain. We've had it drilled into us from grade school that exercise can boost everything from heart health to better buns. But let's discuss why making it one of your first habits of the day is such a stellar move.

Most of us are aware that exercise is great for the body, but did you know that it's also just as powerful for the mind? In fact, exercise gives you mind-boosting super-powers. Ok, so super-powers might be a bit of a stretch, but research does show that exercising increases blood flow to the brain, boosting your ability to think clearly and make good decisions – something you'll need for the rest of your day to be successful.

Jen Hoffman of the online yoga program HealthyMoving.com makes a.m. exercise a part of her daily routine, not only to keep her body healthy but to keep her mind sharp, as well. "I love to start my day with a brisk walk. I've long found it to help me do important critical thinking and problem solving. And now there's research to explain why! We get increased brain blood flow during moderate exercise," she explains, citing an article from the *Journal of Applied*

Physiology, wherein researchers measured cerebral blood flow during exercise. They found that moderate exercise did indeed increase blood flow to the brain, fostering better critical thinking skills and mental alertness.

Why Before 8 a.m.?

Ever had something you intended to get done for the day, but you didn't *quite* get to it? As in, "I meant to bake those three dozen chocolate cupcakes for my son's school Valentine's Day party, but after walking the dog, making dinner, and picking up milk, it just didn't happen." While all of our top priorities are susceptible to being lost in the daily shuffle, exercise seems to be particularly prone to this problem.

Most likely that's because we think exercise is one of those things that we tend to feel we need to devote a lengthy amount of time to (we'll debunk that myth in a moment), as well as the fact that it takes a certain amount of physical energy to complete a workout. If you wait until after a grueling day at the office or chauffeuring the kids around, it might be more difficult to put in the effort, even if you still have the motivation.

Getting a workout in the a.m. doesn't just ensure that we tackle this habit before our day gets away from us. Exercising also revs up the metabolism *all day long.* Pop quiz: Do you want to boost your metabolism first thing in the morning so you can burn calories more efficiently all day, or would you rather keep your metabolism under wraps, sluggishly plugging along, only to shoot up during a quick workout just in time for you to ...go to sleep? I hope the answer is obvious. The best type of workouts to wake up the metabolism include strength-training exercises: toning and lifting weights. But even a quick walk in the morning will still help to wake up the body and mind and set you on the course for success all day long.

But there is another reason exercising in the a.m. is such a powerful habit: Hormones (I told you, they control everything!). Sorry if all this talk about hormones has you feeling like you're back in high school sex-ed, but we just can't get away from them. The fact is, most of us grew up thinking that exercise burned calories, and that burning calories was the key to losing weight. New research shows, however, that our hormones have a lot more to do with weight loss than we once thought. Have you felt like you were spending countless hours at the gym only to see the scale refuse to budge? You can blame your hormones. The good news, though, is that exercise has a regulating effect on our hormones, including the stress hormone, cortisol.

We talked about how eating a healthy breakfast high in protein can also help keep cortisol in check. You might be interested to know that out-of-control cortisol plays a major role in fat storage. If you want to keep your weight in check, keeping your cortisol in check is vital. And exercise can help you accomplish this.

One word of caution here. Make sure to assess your fitness level, especially if you are just starting out on a workout program. Long, exhausting workouts do more than make you feel drained mentally. They can have the opposite effect of what you are striving for, throwing hormones off-kilter and making it even more difficult to lose weight and gain healthy muscle mass. Starting slowly will not only keep your motivation going strong, but it will also keep your hormones going strong, as well!

Cortisol isn't the only hormone affected by exercise. When you exercise, feel-good hormones known as endorphins are released in the brain. Endorphins are like your body's own little mind-altering drug, increasing the sensation of pleasure while minimizing pain. It's probably no surprise, then, that exercise can reduce our levels of stress and improve our mood by flooding our brains with this happy hormone. By starting our day with exercise, we'll be better prepared to face the day with a positive outlook. So slip on the Spandex and make it a habit!

Making it a Habit

In order to make exercise a habit, we have to remember how habit formation works. First, we need a trigger. Your trigger could be to lay out your workout clothes and shoes so they are ready to put on as soon as you wake up. Find an online accountability group or enlist a friend to meet up with you for your morning walk; you'll be less likely to hit the snooze button when you know she's going to be waiting at the corner for you. Use a FitBit or other fitness-tracker device; seeing your progress in black and white is a huge motivator for many people. Find a trigger that works for you and exercising first thing in the morning will soon be easy as pie!

If exercise is new to you and (let's be honest) you aren't exactly looking forward to it, let me give you a few practical suggestions. In her book, *Surprisingly...Unstuck*, Maria Brilaki outlines the exact habit formation program she uses to help her clients make fitness a daily routine. Maria's suggestion is to start small – *really small.* As in, "When the alarm clock goes off (cue) I'm going to get out of bed and do five jumping jacks (habit)."

She calls these habit-forming behaviors "Ridiculously Small Steps" and contends that they work so well because they bypass your conscious mind and address your habits directly. Don't be fooled by how simple these simple steps are. We've been conditioned to believe No Pain, No Gain, and other such nonsense, when in fact, the opposite proves to be true.

When exercisers enjoy the activity, it gives them the motivation they need to keep doing it. The No Pain, No Gain mentality is doomed to failure. Being forced to do something you don't enjoy will only last so long before your mind decides to override its own best intentions and move back toward your comfort zone.

Maria goes on to say that it is only the habits you *enjoy* that will stick with you for the long haul. Don't worry about these habits being too small to have much impact on your fitness level. You will find, to your amazement, that as you stick with your Ridiculously Small Steps, over time your exercise habit will grow! Let's go over a few practical suggestions for making morning exercise a habit you can stick with.

Take Action! Ideas for a Morning Exercise Routine

- **Start with Walking.** If you're brand-spanking new to exercise, walking is a great place to start. Just commit to walking around the perimeter of your home and work up from there!

- **Use workout DVDs** such as *BurstFit.* These toning videos use the power of interval training to get results fast. Why work out for 40 minutes when you can work out smart for half the time and get the same results? The ease of being able to work out quickly at home is appealing to many.

- **Work out with a friend.** Accountability will help keep you on track. Just make sure your partner is as committed as you are. A chronic canceller won't help you reach your goals!

- **Try Yoga or Tai Chi.** These exercises are both invigorating and relaxing at the same time. These more gentle forms of exercise may be an especially good choice for those with joint pain or breathing difficulties.

- **Invest in a gym membership**. For some, the pull of knowing you've invested your hard-earned money into something is motivation enough to follow through. Just don't forget to have your workout clothes, car keys, and water bottle ready and waiting as soon as you awaken: they'll be your cue to get to the gym!

- **One last thing** – Don't forget to make it fun! Do something you enjoy and be sure to celebrate your success every time you work out, even if it's just to remind yourself how stinkin' awesome you are for following through with your morning routine, and how hot you're going to look lounging by the pool this summer.

In your workbook, write out your trigger, your exercise routine, and your reward. Be sure to check out the resources in the workbook for more awesome suggestions!

CHAPTER 9
PICK YOUR FIVE

The five habits we've just discussed are all widely used by the highly successful, but they're not the only ones. In fact, your five habits can be whatever suits you best. Here's my secret: I don't exercise by 8 a.m. every morning, other than my five-minute yoga routine to help me wake up. But, I DO exercise every day – it's a habit, and one that has been life-long for me. It's not going anywhere. I just don't make time to do it in the morning.

My five habits?

1. Speak out my Affirmations
2. Read my Goals
3. Map out my day (I call this setting my daily goals and making my to do list)
4. Spend time with God, reading scripture and praying
5. Write down my three Daily Gratitudes (three things I'm thankful for that day)

Terri Savelle Foy, author of *Imagine Big*, shares on her weekly podcast that when she first decided to turn her life around from living paycheck to paycheck to a life of abundance, she started with five habits she would complete every day. For her these included: pray, read something from the Bible, listen to a faith-building message, review her dreams and goals, and finally, exercise.

At the time Terri decided to start a morning routine, she was separated from her husband, stuck at the same income level she had been at for years, and feeling distant in her relationship with God. Realizing she needed to turn things around, she made a commitment to do these five things for 21 days. Thirteen years later, she's still doing them.

They don't sound like all that much, do they? But Terri is now the CEO of a worldwide ministry, and a highly sought-after speaker and coach who is living in her dream home with her husband (who she now has a great marriage with). Just imagine what a morning routine can do for you!

World tennis pro Novak Djokovic outlines the routine he goes through each day to stay on top of his game. He starts with drinking a glass of water and a 20-minute stretching routine, and then makes time for a super-healthy breakfast before he meets his coach to start his training routine. Your routine might not include playing tennis for hours each morning, but it should reflect those habits that will guide you to where you want to be.

So what will your five habits be? If you're still not sure, let me give you a few more ideas that might work well for you.

- **Write.** If you are a writer, blogger, speaker (or want to be!) then spending time letting your creative juices flow first thing in the a.m. will help you get your thoughts in order. I find the quiet of the morning is a great time to write before the distractions of the day (i.e. kids) start to pull my mind in too many directions and I lose focus.

- **Meet up with your accountability partner.** Having a friend who is focusing on the same forward motion in life that you are is a great way to grow in your success journey. By making time to plan, strategize, and bounce ideas off of each other while you work out together, you can kill two birds with one stone! Plan a 15-minute accountability call each morning or make time to share your goals for the day while taking a quick walk.

- **Journal.** Many successful folks know the value of journaling to help them focus their thoughts and intentions for the day. I mentioned that I take time to write down my top three gratitudes for the day. I usually then go on to journal any thoughts that are taking up residence in my head. I've found this to be a great way to solve problems and find answers to questions. Something about writing your thoughts out with pen and paper helps you to get clear on what action you need to take.

- **Reflect.** *Slight Edge* author Jeff Olson recommends rather than thinking about what you are going to do, that you take time to write down what you *did* do. Take a few minutes in the morning to reflect over the day before. After all, as Olson puts it so succinctly, doing things won't create success. Doing the *right* things will. Take time to inventory your previous day and ask yourself if you did the right things. I especially love this practice because it helps keep your focus on the positive, forward momentum rather than focusing on the one or two things you didn't do so well. So you broke down and ate a Snickers bar at 3 p.m? Instead of focusing on that, remind yourself of that healthy breakfast and lunch you ate, and the great workout you got in that morning! Reflecting on your progress will shift your perspective and keep your motivation going strong. I always tended to focus in on the negative things I felt like I didn't accomplish until I put this habit in place. When I started reflecting on what I did do right, I was amazed at how much better I felt about myself and how that feeling kept me moving forward towards my goals.

- **Think.** Many of the world's most successful entrepreneurs will tell you they take time each day to think. Remember Peter Daniels from Chapter Six? He attributes his success to the fact that he sets aside one day every week to think, saying, "I scheduled time to just think. In fact, I reserve one day a week to just think. All my greatest ideas, opportunities, and money-making ventures started with the days I took off to think." You may not be able to set aside an entire day each week just to think, but even five to ten minutes every morning can pay rich dividends in your eventual success.

- **Express gratitude**. The successful know that expressing gratitude is a sure-fire way to reach for the top. Write down three things you are grateful for today. I already mentioned that I make time to write down my three Daily Gratitudes each morning. Or spend a few minutes in prayer, thanking God for whatever blessings come to mind.

- **Write a thank-you note**. Another way to express gratitude is to write one thank-you note or email each day. Many successful people have utilized this technique, including Facebook CEO Mark Zuckerberg, who made it his personal goal in 2014 to write at least one thank-you note every day that year.

- **Use Affirmations.** A powerful way to move towards your goals is to utilize affirmations in your daily success routine. Affirmations are simply statements that affirm your goal as already being accomplished. For example, "I am enjoying reaching my perfect weight of 135 lbs." Be sure to stand in front of a mirror and speak your affirmation to yourself out loud. You believe yourself more than you believe anyone else, so say it loud and clear!

- **Write out your top goals by hand – every day.** This is a quick way to solidify your goals in your mind, and it's a way of proving that you are seriously committed to making your goals a reality. Simply pick your top goals and write them down each day. Many success coaches recommend writing your goals each day for 30 days. Want to show you are really serious about reaching those goals? Don't stop after 30 days. Why not write your yearly goals out each day for 365 days? You might be surprised by the results.

- **Map out your day.** Take time after reviewing your goals to map out your day and you'll be that much closer to achieving the success you crave. After all, having a successful life comes from having successful days. So grab your planner and set up your day. First, pencil in any appointments and commitments that are set in stone. From there, start with your three biggest goals and schedule some time to work on them, preferably in the a.m., of course! Make sure to put down a specific time to work on the goal. Instead of penciling "Exercise" into your planner, write out something like, "6 a.m.- Meet Amy for a 20 minute walk."

- **Take Time to Look Your Best.** Yes, vain as it sounds, taking the time to include morning rituals that make you look and feel your best can have a huge impact on your productivity. You know the difference you feel when you dress up for a night on the town with friends. A little more confident. Bolder. More sure of yourself. Why not take that confidence each day instead of saving it for special occasions? I'm not talking about dressing up like you're heading to your first prom, and of course we know clothes don't make the man, either. Just take the time to put on a shirt that you know complements your figure and wasn't just pulled from the dryer a wrinkled mess! Add a small touch that makes you happy, like a piece of jewelry or a touch of lipgloss (for the ladies, of course!).

One more thing: Whatever your five habits are, don't make your morning routine an overwhelming or time-consuming task that you feel like a slave to. Yes, I'm going to keep harping on simplicity. Don't forget when we talked about how to form good habits! Make sure this is fun and doable. Even if you only work out for five minutes in the morning, like me (ok, ok, my yoga routine *is* technically a workout), you are STILL working out!

Start where you are at and build momentum rather than trying to force yourself to wake up at 4:30 am every day to spend hours reading and exercising, especially if you are used to sleeping in until closer to 8.... Sometimes when I'm rushed, my morning routine only takes me 20 minutes, but the point is that I do it EVERY DAY.

CHAPTER 10
SAMPLE SCHEDULES

I trust that by now you are convinced that adding 5 things to your morning can be simple, doable and fun. If, however, you are wondering how you will add even one more thing to your already rushed morning, allow me show you just how easy it can be.

First of all, let's talk mindset. If you're looking at the addition of a routine as a chore that you need to squeeze into your already overbooked morning, I can almost guarantee you are destined to fail. The key to making your routine stick is to make it something you look forward to each morning. Something you crave. Think of it as a little "me" time that you can use to center yourself and find your focus before your day gets crazy. I've provided a few examples of how you can maximize your morning routine without overwhelming yourself.

The Stay At Home Mom

Lisa dreams of writing her first novel, but as a busy stay-at-home mom she doesn't know when she will ever find the time. Just getting a shower in every morning feels like a major chore at this point! However, Lisa could benefit from a morning routine more than most people. As Lisa will find, the more hectic her day is, the more centering a routine will be.

Lisa is great at jotting down a To Do list each morning that helps her focus on what she needs to accomplish for the day. She loves to spend a few minutes in prayer each morning, as well, but she's found that making time to nourish herself spiritually through scripture reading has been a goal she often falls short of. Lisa could benefit from a morning routine that incorporates the following 5 things:

- **Read for 10 minutes**, focusing on something inspirational, such as a devotion for moms.

- **Use affirmations.** Raising small children can often feel like a thankless job. It's hard to measure your "progress" as a mom when all you see when you look around is a messy house and even messier children. That doesn't mean her day isn't spent making significant strides toward a worthy goal. It just may not feel like it. Affirmations are a great way to keep things in perspective. Lisa's affirmations could include her worth as a mother and wife as well as getting in front of a mirror, looking herself in the eye, and telling herself, "You *are* a successful author!"

- **Write.** Even if it's only 100 words. By breaking her large goal of writing a novel into a small goal of writing each day, Lisa will be surprised how much she can accomplish!

- **Exercise.** A 20-minute walk around the block before her kiddos wake up would give Lisa some time to do something for herself. On days when it's too cold to head outside, a 20-minute interval training DVD does the trick!

- **Eat a Healthy Breakfast**. Moms tend to be notorious for putting themselves last while caring for others and taking the time for a healthy meal is one of the first things to get pushed to the backburner. Why not sit down to a simple breakfast of scrambled eggs and veggies with the kiddos instead of acting like a short order cook/waitress instead?

The Busy Executive

Scott's alarm clock goes off at 5 a.m. and this busy executive doesn't have time to hit the snooze button! With his workout clothes already waiting for him, he heads to the gym for an intense 45-minute workout with weights and the elliptical machine. After a quick shower and a healthy breakfast (that he prepped the night before), Scott heads to the office early so he can complete his routine before anyone else arrives.

While Scott does a great job of making his health a priority, he's feeling a little lost when it comes to getting ahead with his career. He'd love to start his own company and spend his days working for himself but the steps to get there seem a little daunting. Scott could really benefit from a morning routine that puts his goals front and center and reminds him of what he really wants from life. Scott's morning routine could be maximized if his 5 things looked something like this:

- **Review his top 3 goals**. This will help Scott stay on track with what he needs to accomplish daily to start moving towards his bigger goals, rather than staying busy with those tasks that only serve to keep at his current level of success.

- **Map out his day,** making sure to keep his top goals in focus. Accomplishing those tasks that are moving him towards his top priorities should be at the top of his daily to do list.

- **Visualize his future.** This will keep Scott on track when the going gets tough. There's nothing like reminding yourself of where you are heading to keep you motivated!

- **Read for 20 minutes**, specifically setting this time aside to read those books that will help him achieve his career goals.

- **Spend 15 minutes with an accountability partner.** Those with big goals will find that having someone there who can keep them on track will pay rich dividends. Ideally, Scott should look for someone who can act in a mentorship role and help him see the bigger picture when the going gets tough.

The Aspiring Co-Ed

Jimmy is a young college student whose first class doesn't start until 9 am. Good thing, since his night classes sometimes don't end until after 9 pm! Jimmy wants more than just the "normal" college experience of hitting a few too many frat parties and skipping classes. This kid has some serious goals!

Unfortunately, he's not 100 percent sure what he needs to focus on to reach them. Thankfully, Jimmy hit the jackpot with his college advisor, who made a few practical suggestions for Jimmy to implement so he can stay focused on what he wants to achieve. After helping Jimmy craft a few well thought out goals that reflect his vision for the future, his advisor showed him how to put a few other success habits into practice, as well. Jimmy's 5 things might look like this:

- **Review Goals.** Instead of drifting through college aimlessly, having goals for the future will help Jimmy stay on track when it comes to planning his classes and reviewing those goals every day will make sure he doesn't lose sight of what's most important.

- **Journal.** With his whole life ahead of him, Jimmy could really benefit from spending time journaling his thoughts and ideas. Putting pen and paper to his thoughts might even help him figure out the direction he wants to take.

- **Express gratitude.** While he's journaling, Jimmy might want to jot down three things he's grateful for each day.

- **Eat a healthy breakfast.** He will need the nutrients to power his brain through those long hours of classes and studying.

- **Exercise.** Avoiding the 'Freshman Fifteen' may be as easy as taking a few laps around the track before class or hitting the weight room with a friend!

As you can see from these examples, a morning routine can be as varied and personal as each individual. If you're still not sure where to start on crafting a morning routine that you love, I'd suggest starting with the five things we've discussed and fashion your routine from there.

Conversely, look at where you are at in life right now. The routine of a busy mom of six will most definitely look different than that of a single girl! Don't get hung up on the logistics. Remember, the point is just to do *something* that moves you down the path toward success – and to do it every day! Before we part ways, I've got one more super important habit to share with you that will set you up for a successful morning routine.

CHAPTER 11
ONE LAST TIP- GO TO BED EARLY

I once saw a meme online about how to take care of yourself that went something like this: "Treat yourself the way you would treat a small child. Feed yourself healthy food and make sure you spend time outside. Put yourself to bed early. Let yourself take naps. Don't say mean things to yourself and don't put yourself in danger." This may just be one of the most profound pieces of advice you'll ever receive. We've already discussed a couple of those ideas. Before we part ways, let's chat about one more success habit you need to make a part of your arsenal. Going to bed early.

I'm sure I won't make anyone's "favorite girl to party with on a Friday night" list for this one, but if you want to live the successful life, you've got to make the sacrifices that successful people do. Besides, I've noticed that going to bed early is all the rage right now, with some bloggers and health professionals even offering online programs and courses on how to make getting to bed on time a top priority. So jump on the bandwagon and I'll show you why successful people are "early to bed and early to rise!"

In case you haven't noticed, sleep is quickly becoming the hottest way to get fit. Some are even putting it ahead of diet and exercise in helping you maintain your weight and fitness levels! Why? In *The Adrenal Reset Diet,* Dr. Christian explains that the amount of sleep an individual gets each night directly affects not only how much you eat, but what you crave and what your body actually does with those calories you consume. And we haven't even touched on what sleep deprivation does to your mental game yet. Let's dive into why successful people hit the hay early.

Why Successful People Go to Bed Early

I remember years ago watching the popular show *The Apprentice* on television, where two groups of high-achieving individuals compete against one another in various challenges. Back then, Donald Trump wasn't a candidate for president; he was a business mogul who held the fate of these people's professional lives in his hands. The last man/woman standing on the show would go on to win an internship with the Donald himself and (hopefully) achieve overwhelming success.

In one episode, a group of competitors was being led by a hard-working (pushy) young woman to renovate a hotel on a tight budget and with major time constraints. Keeping her team up round the clock to finish the project, she worked them like dogs, hoping to achieve a better outcome than their challengers.

When it came time to face Trump and his team in the boardroom, the young woman leading her team proudly told Trump that working her team to the bone without giving them time to sleep was a work ethic learned from her dad, who would often say, "Did you have time to sleep? Then you had time to work." Maybe she was trying to impress Trump, who reportedly only sleeps three hours a night, with her sleep-shunning skills. Unfortunately, her plan didn't work out so well. She didn't make it out of the boardroom before the famous words "You're fired!" were aimed in her direction.

Sadly, the work ethic that drives people to shun sleep is far too prevalent in our society. Many people think foregoing sleep in favor of "getting more done" or even mindlessly flipping through television programs is a badge of honor. If you know what successful people do, however, you'll be sure to make sleep a high priority.

In her definitive guide on sleep, aptly named *Go to Bed*, Sarah Ballantyne, PhD and founder of thepaleomom.com, gives us the lowdown on the detriments of too little sleep. These include the effects of sleep on cognitive functions such as attention, decision making, and memory. You know, those pesky little mental processes we all need to focus on our goals and make things happen? When we shun sleep for other activities, our cortisol levels rise, and we already know what that does to the rest of our body functions! From fat storage to mental clarity, keeping cortisol in check is a must, and getting a good night's sleep is one of the key ways to do it.

If you want to follow in the footsteps of high achievers like Bill Gates, Arianna Huffington, and Jeff Bezos, be sure to make sleep a top priority. These super successful folks make sure to get plenty of rest, logging at least seven hours a night.

Making It a Habit

If you're used to piddling your evening hours away on worthless pursuits (like, say binge-watching sitcoms while throwing back salty snacks on the couch), don't despair at the thought of getting to bed early. You're one of the top 3 percent now, remember? You are a success in the making, and adopting the habits of the successful is a price you're willing to pay.

Tom Rath makes a great case for getting your z's in his book *Eat, Move, Sleep*. "Think of sleep as an investment rather than an expense," he explains. This subtle mind shift will keep you from resenting your early bed time like a cranky toddler when 8 pm rolls around. Learn to think of sleep as important to your well-being and and guard your bed time carefully. Guarding your rest is the same as guarding your productivity. Don't make the mistake of our lovely *Apprentice* contestant and sacrifice sleep for hours of zombie-like wheel-spinning. Think of sleep as just another rung on the ladder to success and you'll be well on your way!

Take Action! Suggestions for a Good Night's Sleep

Boosting the quality of sleep you get each night is just as important as making sure to get enough hours of sleep. Let's go over some simple things you can do to make sure those hours are the most restful they can be by getting rid of sleep hindrances and creating some relaxing bedtime rituals.

- **Turn off the tablet**. *Yeah, I said it*. I know you spend more nights than you might care to admit mindlessly scrolling through your Facebook feed until well after 11 p.m. Do yourself a favor and leave the electronic devices out of the bedroom. I mean *all* electronic devices, for that matter. As Dr. Ballantyne so quaintly puts it, the bedroom should be reserved for sex and sleeping, so even the TV should find a new address in another room. It's a distraction you don't need if you're going to skyrocket to success.

- **Try climate control.** Dr. Christianson recommends keeping your bedroom cool, setting your thermostat to the mid-60s. Try taking a warm bath before slipping into bed. The heat from the tub followed by the subsequent dip in temperature will signal to your body that it's time for sleep.

- **Carbs before bed.** Remember when we talked about how important eating a healthy, high-protein breakfast was for your daily productivity? If you were mourning the loss of your favorite carbs for breakfast, you can rejoice! According to Dr. Christianson, your insulin response peaks around dinner time, making this the ideal to time for some carbohydrates. Having a healthy dose of carbs for dinner will keep blood sugar levels in check, and cortisol won't be able to rear its ugly head, causing icky sleep disturbances like waking up at 3 am. Think complex carbs, such as sweet potatoes, beans and squash and you'll be sleeping like a baby!

- **Reflect**. Taking a few minutes at the end of the day to jot down any thoughts or ideas you still have running around in your head is a great way to clear your mind before bed. I often like to take a few minutes each evening to reflect on my day, jotting down the things I accomplished that day that moved me closer to my goals. This technique, by the way, is great for keeping your motivation high and keeping your progress right before your eyes.

- **Give aromatherapy a go**. Scent has a powerful effect on the brain. Your sense of smell is directly processed by your deep limbic system, the same area that regulates sleep cycles. Scents such as lavender, Roman chamomile, or cedarwood essential oils have a calming effect on the mind and have been widely used to promote a good night's rest. Pick up a diffuser that circulates the oil throughout the air in your bedroom, or simply inhale a few drops directly from the bottle before going to bed.

- **Cut the lights.** All the lights! Most sleep experts recommend making your sleeping area as dark as possible, even covering up lights from electronic devices and alarm clocks, as well as using black-out curtains to curtail any light coming from street lights.

- **Try amber glasses.** If you are still struggling with sleep, or just want to take every step possible to ensure a good night's sleep (and you don't mind spending your evenings looking like a dork), you may want to try using amber glasses. Amber glasses can block blue light that signals our body to stay awake by blocking melatonin production in the brain.

By now I hope you're eager to hit the hay early so you can enjoy amazing productivity each morning! Be sure to head on over to the workbook and jot down a few changes you plan to make to your bedtime routine to upgrade your sleep quality. If going to bed at a decent time is a major change for you, make a plan to go to bed half an hour earlier each week until you reach your desired bedtime.

I've enjoyed sharing the five things successful people do before 8 a.m. with you (and the one thing they do each night!) I know how powerful these habits are in transforming lives; not just the lives in the stories I've shared with you throughout this book, but your life as well. Take these habits and make them your own. Put your own spin on them. Be sure to incorporate the tips I've shared with you on making easy changes. After all, it's only the things you *do* that will change you!

ABOUT THE AUTHOR

Michelle is a little obsessed with living life to the full. Having struggled with her own health issues, including thyroid disease and gut dysbiosis. Michelle finally determined to do whatever it took to regain her health and energy.

A Certified Transformational Nutrition Coach and best-selling author, Michelle now helps women rebalance their hormones and regain their energy so they can give irritability, depression and exhaustion the boot and finally feel energetic, joyful and ready to take on life. Find her at overcomingauto.com.